Birds Do the
Strangest Things

For Deborah Hornblow

To Anna and Nathaniel,
and in memory of my father, Arthur Singer,
whose love of art and nature I share,
and whose encouragement I enjoyed

First paperback edition, 1991
Revised edition

Text copyright © 1965, 1991 by Random House, Inc. Illustrations copyright © 1991 by Alan D. Singer. All rights reserved under International and Pan-American Copyright Conventions. Published in the United States by Random House, Inc., New York, and simultaneously in Canada by Random House of Canada Limited, Toronto.

Library of Congress Cataloging-in-Publication Data
Hornblow, Leonora, 1920– Birds do the strangest things / by Leonora and Arthur Hornblow ; illustrations by Alan D. Singer. p. cm. —(Step-up nature books) Summary: Describes twenty-two birds with unusual habits or characteristics, including the ostrich, kiwi, honey guide, and hornbill. ISBN 0-679-81159-1 (pbk.)—ISBN 0-679-91159-6 (lib. bdg.)
1. Birds—Juvenile literature. [1. Birds.] I. Hornblow, Arthur, 1893– . II. Singer, Alan D., ill. III. Title. QL676.2.H67 1991 598.251—dc20 90-8583 CIP AC

Manufactured in the United States of America 1 2 3 4 5 6 7 8 9 10

Birds Do the Strangest Things

By Leonora and Arthur Hornblow

Illustrated by Alan D. Singer

Revised Edition

STEP-UP BOOKS

Random House New York

CONTENTS

1

THE BIGGEST

On the sandy grasslands of Africa lives the world's biggest bird. It is the ostrich. Some ostriches grow to be eight feet tall. They all have long, thin necks. They all have long, strong legs. And very strange birds they are. The biggest birds in the world cannot fly.

Zebras and antelopes like to walk along with ostriches. The ostrich is so tall that it is easy for him to watch out for enemies.

When an ostrich sees an enemy, he runs. This tells the antelopes and zebras that they should run, too. Ostriches can run

fast. An enemy might never catch an ostrich if he did not do a strange thing.
Often he just runs around in big circles.
If he is caught, he fights. He fights
with his feet. He can kill an enemy with
one kick.

The ostrich does not fight his friends,

the zebra and the antelope. They kick up many small animals and insects as they walk. These are things the ostrich likes to eat.

The female ostrich is not as big as the male. Nor is she as pretty. She is sandy gray. Her color helps to hide her when she sits on her eggs in the sand. Several females share a nest with one male. There may be 20 huge eggs in one nest. A female sits on the eggs if the day is cold. At night the male sits on the eggs.

There is a story that ostriches bury their heads in the sand to hide from an enemy. Ostriches would never do such a silly thing. They may rest their heads on the sand while they are sitting on their eggs. Then it is not easy for them to see an enemy. Maybe they hope an enemy can't see them.

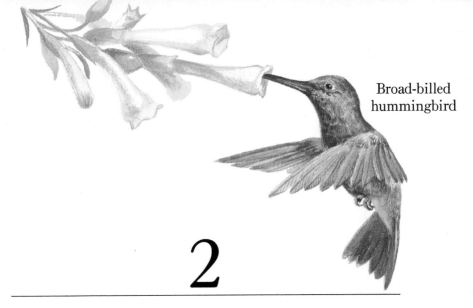

Broad-billed
hummingbird

2

THE FLYING JEWEL

The hummingbird is the only bird that can fly backward. He can fly straight up and down and sideways, too. He can even fly when he is upside down! And perhaps strangest of all, he can fly without going anywhere. He is like a tiny helicopter.

Hummingbirds are the smallest birds in the world. There are many kinds, and they are all beautiful. They are like jewels with wings. Though they are tiny, they are very bold.

A hummingbird seems to know that his enemies cannot catch him. He will fight anything. He can even scare away a hawk.

A hummingbird eats 50 or 60 meals a day. He flashes from flower to flower. He sticks his long bill into a flower and sips the nectar. The hummingbird also eats small insects he finds in the flower. The insects and the sugar in nectar give the little birds their great strength and energy.

The ruby-throated hummingbird needs all the strength and energy he can get. For every winter this hummingbird makes an amazing flight. First he eats and eats to store up food. He gets quite fat. Then he leaves home. Off he flies for days and days. He flies 500 miles across the ocean to get to a warm place. No one knows how so small a bird can fly so far without food or rest. But the ruby-throat does it every year.

Magnificent
hummingbird

Ruby-throated
hummingbird

Bigger birds can fly farther. But the ruby-throat is less than four inches long.

The ostrich is the biggest bird. He is a good walker and a great runner. But he cannot fly at all. It is strange that the smallest bird flies everywhere. Even to move an inch he flies. He cannot walk. He does not have to. He can get there faster with those wonderful wings.

Male
ruby-throat

Female
ruby-throat

3

BIRD ABOUT TOWN

If you live in a city, you have probably seen a pigeon. You may have fed pigeons popcorn in the park. You may have seen them getting under people's feet in the street.

Pigeons have lived near humans for at least 5,000 years. At first people used them for food. Then they found out a strange thing. Some pigeons, when taken far away from their nests, flew right back. This gave someone a good idea. Maybe the pigeon could bring a message back with him. Many, many pigeons have been trained to do this. They are called homing pigeons. A homing pigeon carries the message in a little tube. The tube is put on the bird's leg.

Before radio, the homing pigeon's most

important use was in war time. Pigeons will fly right through smoke and gun-fire. They will fly anywhere. Some pigeons have been given medals for bravery by the army. Pigeons don't care about medals. All they want is to get home.

4

THE FLYING SUBMARINE

The loon is the best swimmer of all the flying birds. He can swim the fastest. He can dive the deepest. He can stay underwater the longest. His legs are set far back on his body. They help him when he is swimming.

The loon is a fine flier, too. He can fly a mile a minute. But he has trouble getting up in the air. He cannot take off from land. He has to run along on top of the water. Sometimes the loon runs for a quarter of a mile to get up enough speed to take off.

He also has a hard time landing. He cannot come down on the water softly. He lands with a great big splash. Loons like to be in the water. They can hardly stand up on land.

But loons have to come out of the water to lay their eggs. They make a nest for their eggs on land.

After the eggs hatch, the baby loons go into the water. Their parents take them. They want to teach the babies to swim. At first, little loons ride around on the grownups' backs. Then the parents slowly sink under the water. Only their heads show. But the babies know that their parents are below them. Soon the little loons learn to swim alone.

One of the strangest things about the loon is his cry. It may sound like a terrible scream for help. Or a ghost laughing on Halloween. It is a very scary sound. There is an old saying, "crazy as a loon." But the only thing crazy about the loon is the noise he makes.

5

KING OF THE AIR

The bald eagle is the mighty hunter of the sky. People have always admired him.

Few birds can fly as high as the eagle. He circles in the air looking for food. When he is a mile up in the sky, he can see a rabbit on the ground. He can see a fish from up there, too. Down he dives to get his food. He rarely misses.

But the mighty eagle is also a thief. He often steals his food from another bird. He waits until the other bird catches a

fish. Then the eagle dives straight at him.
The other bird is often frightened by the
eagle. So he drops his fish. The eagle will
catch the fish before it hits the ground.
Then back he flies to his huge high nest
to enjoy his stolen supper.

6

THE ODD ONE

There are many birds that cannot fly. But the kiwi is the only bird that doesn't have wings. His feathers are strange, too. They look like hair. Hidden under the hairy feathers are two small knobs. Maybe these knobs were wings long ago.

Kiwis live underground at the bottom of trees. They dig holes to live in. The female kiwi lays her eggs in the hole. A kiwi is only as big as a chicken. But each egg weighs almost a whole pound.

A kiwi does not leave his underground home until night comes. Then he goes out hunting for his favorite food—worms. His long bill is a marvelous tool for worm hunting. The kiwi moves around in the dark, smelling the ground. He can smell a worm down below. He stamps with his big feet. The worm comes up to see what is happening. Good-bye, worm!

Kiwis are found only in New Zealand. They may not be beautiful birds, but they surely are strange.

7

THE LONE BANDIT

No one likes a shrike—probably not even other shrikes. He is a small bird with a hooked beak. He has a band of black feathers around his eyes. This makes him look like a bandit. He acts like a bandit, too. He sits and waits for a mouse, a frog, a snake, or another bird to pass by. Almost anything looks fine to him. Even another shrike. He hits it with his sharp beak. It falls to the ground. Then the shrike does a very strange thing. He picks it up with his beak. He flies with it to a thorny bush. If there is no bush, he may take it to a barbed-wire fence. He always hangs up his prey, the way a butcher hangs up his meat. This is why he is sometimes called the butcherbird.

The butcherbird often eats what he has hung up, right away. But if there is more to capture, he does not always stop to eat. He flies away to look for more. Maybe he wants to be sure that there is always food in his butcher shop.

8

THE BUILDER

Can you believe that a bird can build a house? Well, there is one that does. When explorers in New Guinea first saw these houses, they thought children had built them. But bowerbirds had built them. What wonderful bowers they are! Many have roofs. Some even have rooms. There are different kinds of bowerbirds. They build different kinds of bowers.

One kind of bowerbird makes a garden of moss around a tree. Then he builds a house of twigs. Sometimes he builds it six feet tall. He puts leaves and moss and ferns all around. He makes little piles of berries, stones, shells, and flowers. When the flowers die, he throws them out and brings fresh ones. Bowerbirds are always looking for colorful things. They will even steal them from another bird's bower.

The blue satin bowerbird starts his bower with a mat of twigs. In the middle of the mat he builds two walls of twigs. The blue satin bowerbird seems to like the color blue. He decorates his bower with blue flowers and blue feathers, blue shells and blueberries. Everything he puts in his house is blue.

Most amazing of all, the blue satin bowerbird can paint the inside of his bower blue. He makes his paint out of charcoal and berry juice. He even makes a paintbrush out of a piece of bark. He holds the brush in his beak.

It may take a bowerbird months to build his bower. He builds the bower to attract a female bowerbird. When a female comes along, the male stops work on the house. He does a dance for her. After a while she goes in to see if she likes the bower.

But the female never uses the bower for

a nest. When the time comes to lay her eggs, she flies away. She makes a plain nest for herself and her eggs. The male, the wonderful builder, does not help her. He does not even know he has children. All he cares about is looking after his bower.

9

THE SILENT HUNTER

Some owls look wise. Some owls look gentle. But don't be fooled by looks. No owl is wise. Nor are any owls gentle.

There are many kinds of owls. Some are as small as sparrows. Others are as big as roosters. Large or small, all owls have sharp, curved claws and strong, hooked beaks. And by nature, all owls are great hunters.

The owl goes out hunting as soon as it is dark. He kills and eats things that walk or fly, crawl or swim. Owls can see the smallest creatures. Owls can hear the smallest creatures. They can see and hear them day or night.

Great
horned
owl

Screech owl

Barn
owl

Snowy owl

Owls use both their eyes and ears when they hunt in the dark, dark night. They see and hear a beetle crawling by. Owls eat a lot of beetles. An owl does not miss a thing. Not even a quiet little mouse.

An owl will kill and eat a skunk. This could be why owls' feathers sometimes have an awful smell. The wing feathers of owls are very soft. Owls can fly right past you without making a sound.

There is another strange thing about owls. They can puff their feathers all up. Then the owls look twice as big as they really are. They do this to show off to their mates. Or to scare enemies away from their nests. ,

An owl looks strange when he is all puffed up. He also looks strange when he is watching something move. He follows it with his eyes. But his eyes can only see straight ahead. So he has to move his whole head. His head seems to turn all the way around and upside down. Sometimes it looks as if he is going to twist it right off!

Owls make all kinds of sounds. But their best-known sound is "hoo-hoo." And who-who wants to be an owl?

Barred owl

Screech owl

10

THE HONEY SCOUT

A little bird called the honey guide lives in Africa. He is always on the lookout for animals or humans who want honey. People in Africa know this. So when they want honey, they look for a honey guide. He always leads them to the nests of honeybees.

The honey guide starts chirping as soon as he sees a hunter. Then off he flies. The hunter follows as fast as he can. If he is slow, the bird waits and chirps even louder.

A honey guide is a very good guide. He flies and chirps to keep a hunter going the right way. When at last they get to the honey, the guide waits. He sits on the tree. He cannot get to the honeycomb by

himself. That is why he brings humans
and other animals to honey. The strange
thing is that he wants the wax in the
honeycomb. Most people and animals
don't want the wax. They want the honey.
So both the hunters and the honey guides
are happy.

11

THE BEACH CLEANER

Herring gulls are called "sea" gulls. Yet they live near lakes and rivers, too. They rarely go far out to sea. Sometimes gulls will follow a ship for miles. Not because they like the sea or the ship. What they like is the leftover food that people throw overboard. Gulls are great garbage collectors.

Most of the time gulls stay around docks and beaches looking for food. When a gull finds something, he eats it. He is always eating.

In fact, a gull will eat almost anything. If a dead fish washes up on the beach, it does not stay there long. The minute a gull sees it, he goes for it. When other gulls see one gull go for something, they go too. Then they usually fight over every scrap. Soon there is nothing left.

That is why gulls are such good friends to people. They help to keep our beaches clean.

Sometimes a gull will find shellfish near the sea. Gulls love shellfish. But a gull cannot open a shellfish with his beak. So he flies with it high up in the air. When he is over some rocks, or a hard road, or even a car, he drops the shellfish. It smashes open. The gull dives down after it. He knows that if he does not get there fast, another gull will eat his shellfish.

There is a strange thing about herring gulls and food. There is one time in their lives when they are fussy about eating. That is when they are babies.

As soon as a baby gull hatches, he looks for something red. Every grown-up gull has a red spot on its beak. The baby pecks at his parent's red spot. His parents won't feed him unless he does. Stranger still, the baby will not eat unless he finds something red to peck. He will just starve.

You can try to feed a baby gull. But first you must show him something red. Almost any red thing will do.

By the time the baby leaves the nest, he is no longer fussy about pecking something red, or about his food. Off he flies to help keep the beaches clean.

12

HAMMER-HEAD

If you watch a woodpecker in the woods, you will see him slowly hopping up the side of a tree. He stops. He puts his head

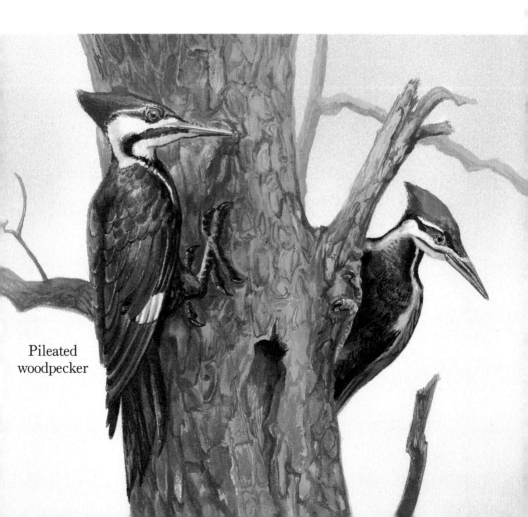

Pileated
woodpecker

to one side. He listens. He is listening for the sounds of insects inside the tree. If he hears any, he leans back on his stiff tail. Then, "rat-a-tat-tat." He pounds with his sharp beak. He makes a small hole in the tree. Into the hole goes his long, sticky tongue. Out come the insects. The woodpecker gets a tasty meal, and helps the tree get rid of pesky bugs.

No other bird can use its head as a hammer. No other bird has such a hard head.

The woodpecker doesn't hammer just to get insects. Hammering is also one of his ways of talking. He has a voice. But usually he hammers on roofs or dead logs to let other woodpeckers know he is there. His hammering will let you know he is there, too. Go have a look at him. He may be hammering a big hole in a tree. When it is big enough, he and a female woodpecker will probably use it as a nest. Some woodpeckers use the same nest for many years in a row. They line the nest with chips of wood. And in it they will raise lots of little hammerheads.

Yellow-shafted flicker

13

THE OILY BIRD

The oilbird loves the dark. He makes his nest inside the darkest cave he can find. Bats live in these same caves with him. Hundreds of oilbirds and bats fly around together in the blackest caves. They never hit anything.

Like the bat, an oilbird can send out signals as he flies. The signal is a ticking sound. The ticking sound hits whatever is in front of him, and then echoes back. The echo tells the oilbird something is ahead.

As soon as the sun goes down, the oilbirds fly out of their caves and into the dark forests. There they eat fruit and nuts from palm trees. These nuts are very oily. Because the oilbird eats nuts all the time, he gets oily, too. That is why he is called the oilbird.

The oilbird will fly for miles looking for food. Sometimes he flies as far as 50 miles. But he is sure to be home again before the sun comes out.

14

THE SHOW-OFF

To win a peahen's attention, the peacock does a strange and wonderful thing. He opens his tail feathers like a great big fan. It is the most remarkable sight in the world of birds.

The peacock seems to know it. He poses for the peahen. He parades like a soldier. And to finish the show, he does a little dance.

The peahen makes believe she does not see him. For a long time she looks the other way. Then she begins a dance of her own. She runs in front of the peacock. And she runs behind him. She does this again and again. Now the peacock knows he has won her with his beauty.

The peacock is a member of the chicken

family. He is prettier. But his little cousin, the chicken, is much more useful to people. In fact, the chicken is perhaps the most useful bird on earth.

Never tell that to a peacock!

15

THE FOOLER

The European cuckoo is one of the birds whose call is its own name. When you hear, "Cuckoo, cuckoo," you know who it is. But a cuckoo can change its call and the way it flies. It can fool you.

Strangest of all is the way it can fool other birds. A female cuckoo puts her eggs in some other bird's nest. She picks the nest of a bird whose eggs are the same color as her eggs. Then she flies away forever. The other poor bird hatches the cuckoo eggs.

When the baby cuckoo hatches, it is almost always bigger than the other babies in the nest. It may even grow bigger than the bird who hatched it. But she still thinks it is her own child. She keeps on feeding it.

As soon as the little cuckoo learns to fly, it leaves the nest. It goes to meet other cuckoos. They may be hundreds of miles away. But the young cuckoo finds them. This is one of the strange things that happen in the world of birds.

16

THE HIDE-AWAY BIRD

There are many kinds of birds' nests. But the strangest of all is the hornbill's.

Two hornbills find a tree with a hole in it. The female climbs in. Then they plaster the front of the hole. They make the plaster out of mud. It is very strong. They leave a little opening. It is just big enough to let the male feed the female. He feeds her while she sits on her eggs. Nothing can get at her or her eggs in her sealed-up nest.

The little hornbills are hatched in the hole. The father feeds his sealed-up family. His tail gets worn from rubbing against the tree. He gets tired and thin. After two or three months the mother breaks out. She is fat and has grown a new set of feathers. She is stiff from sit-ting in such a small place. But she takes over the feeding of the babies.

It is hard to believe that sometimes the babies plaster themselves back into the hole. Not the mother. She is glad to be out.

17

ALL DRESSED UP

The penguin looks funny and friendly. His feathers are black and white. So it seems as if he is wearing a neat little suit and a white shirt. He stands up straight on his short legs. He looks like a little person all dressed up.

Not all penguins are little. The biggest is the emperor penguin. He may grow to be four feet tall.

The emperor penguin lives near the South Pole, far, far away from people. It is always cold there. In his whole life the emperor never touches dry land! He is always on the ice and snow, or in the cold water.

It is a wonderful sight to see penguins marching across the ice. They usually waddle along in a line, one by one. Sometimes they drop down on their stomachs and push themselves along with their feet and wings. They can go quite fast. They zip along on the ice and snow like sleds. It must be fun.

There is a long, dark night near the South Pole. The sun does not shine for half the year. This is when the mother penguin lays her eggs. Emperor penguins do not have nests. As soon as the egg is laid, the father puts it on his feet. He holds it to keep it from freezing on the ice. He does not leave the egg for a moment. The father's warm feathers and belly cover the egg like a blanket. For two months he holds it.

The coldest winds on earth blow around him. But he hardly moves. And he does not eat. When the little penguin hatches, the mother takes over. She has spent the last two months feeding at sea. Now she will help to look after the baby. At last the hungry father can get something to eat. Soon the little penguin can waddle about. Then all the parents gather all the children together in a big "kindergarten." The big penguins stand around the little ones. They make a fence of grown-up penguins. This helps to keep some of the snow and wind away from the young ones.

The little penguins will never learn to

fly. Penguins' wings are too small. But penguins are wonderful swimmers. And their wings help them in the cold, rough sea. They play in the waves. They dive for food. But they don't stay under very long. They have to come up for air.

The penguin has a strange way of getting out of the water. He dives down under the water. Then he swims toward the shore as fast as he can. Just before he reaches the land, he jumps out.

He may jump six feet in the air. But he always lands on his feet. He goes back in the water when he gets hungry. He does not know how to eat on land. This can make life hard for a penguin if he is taken to a zoo. He has to be taught to eat the fish that are thrown to him or given to him. Sometimes this takes weeks. But he always learns.

18

DADDY-LONGLEGS

High on the roofs of many houses in Europe there are huge nests. They are the nests of beautiful white storks. Some of the storks return to the same nests year after year. They are wonderful to watch as they come and go.

One stork stays in the nest to watch over the baby storks. The other goes off looking for food. The stork in the nest watches the sky, waiting for the other one to come home. When they meet again, they do a strange and wonderful thing. The stork in the nest stands up and rattles its beak. The other stork rattles its beak in answer. They bow to each other. They twist their necks back and around and about. This is their way of talking. For they have no voices at all.

The storks live in their roof nests all through the summer. But when the cold days begin, they meet out in the fields. There they stand. They rattle their bills for a long time.

Then suddenly they rise high in the air. They are off on one of the greatest trips in the world of birds. The young storks leave first. They have never taken this trip before. There is no one to show them the way. But they know just where they are going. They are going to Africa, 6,000 miles away.

The people are sad to see them go. They love to have the storks living upon their roofs. They believe that it is good luck to have a stork on their house.

Some people put big baskets and wagon wheels on their roofs. They hope the storks will build nests in them when they come back. If they do, the people are very happy. It is fun to have another family on the roof.

19

BYE-BYE, BIRDIE

The world is full of birds. Some of them are around all the time. Others, like the swallow, come and go.

Male birds are usually more colorful than females. And they usually sing the most. We love to listen to them. But they are not singing for us. They are talking to other birds. A male goldfinch seems to sing to a female goldfinch, "Look at me. I am pretty." If she agrees, she makes a nest while he sings. But most bird songs are warning songs. Many birds, like robins and orioles, take certain trees for themselves. A robin's song may really be a call to a blue jay, "Keep out! This is my tree."

One bird with a very loud call is the crow. Not all people like crows. They put up scarecrows to keep crows away from gardens. But scarecrows don't always scare crows. The crows sit right on them and say, "Caw-caw-caw." They seem to be laughing. Could they be laughing at us? After all, people are strange and wonderful, too.